Vote Like a Boss

Vote Like a Boss

An Entrepreneur's Perspective on Innovation, Leadership, Creativity, Storytelling, and Voting

Tiffany Ann Norwood

Tribetan Press

This book is dedicated to all the bosses past, present, and future- who spoke up, stood up, showed up and Voted.

Thank you for making the world a better place for us all.

CONTENTS

Title Page

Title Page

Copyright

Dedication

Acknowledgments   3

Foreword   5

Preface   9

Introduction   13

::: THE SPEECH :::   17

A Cat   21

The Power of We 1.0   25

That Tree in the Forest   31

Persuasive Storytelling for Changemakers   35

Vote Like a Boss   43

Astound Yourself   53

The Power of We 2.0   57

That Unicorn   63

Hermione Rising   67

::: INSPIRATION :::   73

A Prayer for Those Inspired   75

Black Lives Matter   81

The Kindness of Strangers   85

::: FINAL THOUGHTS :::   89

Afterword   91

More Vote Like a Boss   95

About Tiffany Norwood   99

"In every moment of your life, you are either a leader or a follower. Make a choice."
James W. Norwood Jr., Father

ACKNOWLEDGMENTS

Thank you to Mary Ann, Adaora, Pastor Beverly, Shola, and others for contributing to Vote Like a Boss. Thank you to Rosie for helping me to launch POET and bringing teachers and students into the innovation discussion.

Thank you to my Mom and Dad for always being supportive of my mad scientist ideas. And to my brother James, I miss you. I submit this manuscript on the anniversary of your death.

Charlie, Amelia, Molly, Jess, Robert, Rebecca, Siobhan, Michael, Ryan, Marin Walter, Abe, and Bruno; my amazing godchildren, thank you in advance for the beautiful future you will help to create...with your vote.

FOREWORD

Every presidential election defines a country, and America's 2020 election is going to be a whopper. It will represent who we are and what we aspire to be in the midst of Black Lives Matter, Me Too movements, climate change, extreme wealth inequities, crumbling global relationships, and so much more. Yet it is the profoundly personal vote that leads to that collective impact.

I will admit my relationship with voting is uneven at best. I've taken it for granted, having grown up in post-civil rights America. As a reporter at ABC News and CNN, I covered many elections, including the historic election of Barack Obama. And, as I covered them, ironically, I often "forgot" to vote.

Traipsing the country, I racked up tens of thousands of miles from Watertown, South Dakota to Sevierville, Tennessee, to Boston, Mass, Seattle, Washington and San Diego, California, dozens of states and dozens and dozens of cities. Staring into the eyes of many thousands of people in the crowds, I always sensed the same longing from each person: to be safe, to find a good job, to care for their families. And, at the same time, divergence. While healthcare is critical, is it a right; while childcare is essential for parents to go to work, is it a right?

I am also a lawyer, which I add only to point out that the law regulates every single part of our lives in some way. The infrastructure for all of it rests in the hands of our elected officials, our local, state, and national leaders. Period. They decide how we live, from what we eat to where we work, to the healthcare we get, to how our children are educated, to the taxes we pay.

And Tiffany Norwood is right. Beyond being a civic duty, voting also has tremendous implications for how seriously we take our opinions and ideas in other areas of our life. It is as she says in Vote Like a Boss, "If we don't think our vote matters, will we think our ideas, dreams or goals matter." Ultimately, she makes the point that "successful people don't waste opportunities to be heard or counted." She speaks to a truth that is TRUTH for all of us- voting is one of the most critical steps in training our inner boss.

I find that ironies and insight often come hand in hand, the double-I; twice the impact, always. Ironically, the most powerful insights, when revealed more often than not, seem blatantly obvious. Voting, choosing to vote, demanding transparency from our leaders, insisting relentlessly that we can ensure that each and every vote is counted are the most critical decisions and actions we can take as Americans. It is both an I and a We as we work towards the country we want to live in today, tomorrow, and beyond.

Adaora Udoji
New York City

PREFACE

I have been asked countless times to write a book. So finally, I did. This book wasn't quite the one people were asking for, nor expecting. I will write that other book about my life someday. To be honest, I am still processing the experience myself.

What if we each got just one other person to vote?

Vote Like a Boss, however, couldn't wait. The moment for it is now. In this election year. In this 100th anniversary year for the 19th Amendment and the 55th for the Voting Rights Act. In this year of racial division and a global pandemic. Giving a new voice and new ideas to inspire my fellow citizens to participate actively in our democracy- is the most important thing.

I thought if I could get one more person to vote, or two or three, it would be worth it. In my mind, if we want to double turn out, it is simple: each of us gets one person who hasn't voted before to vote this year. Just like with startups, it's the consistent small steps forward that lead to significant progress. *Vote Like a Boss* is my small step.

Tiffany Norwood
Washington, DC

"Regret is more painful than failure."

Tiffany Norwood

INTRODUCTION

In the 1990s, at the age of 27, Tiffany Norwood did something that no other entrepreneur has done since -she raised over $670 million dollars to fund a startup. That money was used to build the first-ever global digital radio platform; launch three satellites into space (including XM Radio); support the development of MP3/MP4 technologies, and invest in a new generation of digital radio receivers.

As one of the first successful black female tech entrepreneurs in the world, Ms. Norwood's career has spanned 52 countries, 30 years, 7 startups, and a patent. She was also the first in her family to be born with all of their civil rights.

Weaving together a unique narrative about innovation and leadership, in *Vote Like A Boss*, Tiffany shares her extraordinary story as a founder and asks herself (and all of us): Could she have been an entrepreneur, inventor, and leader if she didn't have the right to vote? And, is voting itself an act of self-worth? Celebrating both the 100th anniversary of the 19th Amendment and the women's right to vote; and the 55th anniversary of the Voting Rights Act, Tiffany talks about why taking yourself seriously like speaking up to family and friends, raising your hand in class; and yes even voting, are all the same personality traits that are critical for success in business, school, sports, and life.

An acclaimed storyteller, Ms. Norwood, has spoken to audiences worldwide, at venues like the European Parliament, Cornell University, Global Entrepreneurship Congress, Yale, and the Creative Business Cup. In *Vote Like a Boss*, Tiffany does the hard work to compel us to consider the human connection as one of our greatest assets, the importance of taking your imagination seriously and showing up like a boss in every part of your life. Beyond the title essay, this collection also includes "The Power of We," the ever-popular "Hermione Rising," and even a short overview of "Persuasive Storytelling."

Vote Like a Boss is a collection of essays, writings, and poems presented and performed by global serial entrepreneur Tiffany Norwood at the US Patent and Trademark Office's 2020 WES in Washington, DC. Given as her last live speech before the pandemic, Tiffany used her platform to speak to the new reality that was coming, the need to look after each other, and the opportunity to reimagine everything.

"Miracles happen through other people."
Tiffany Norwood

::: THE SPEECH :::

The following is a collection of essays, writings and poems performed in front of a live audience. Please read as spoken word.

A CAT

What a great day to be in such an inventive space, celebrating and sharing genius.

So, this is what I was thinking. I'm going to start by talking about Billionaires. Then tell you my story, chat about taking yourself seriously, voting and being persuasive. I will finish off with math, economics, and unicorns.

I might even throw in a cat.

Actually, let's start with the cat. Schrödinger's cat, to be specific. You know the one in the box.

The experiment goes something like this. There is a cat in a box. Is it alive or dead?

Well, according to Schrödinger, both.

Until we open the box, the cat is whatever we imagine it to be. If we imagine it to be dead, done, it is dead. If we imagine it to be alive, done, it is alive.

We hold the power of life and death over that cat, just with our thoughts.

Let me share with you some of mine.

"It all seems impossible until it is done."
Nelson Mandela

THE POWER OF WE 1.0

And when I talk about Billionaires, I am talking about you.

You are a Billionaire, right here, right now, today, this moment, sitting in this room.

You are a Billionaire!

I am speaking about you, you, you, and you too.

Everyone in this space. The 12,000 others on this campus, the more than one million around the country
and the world that will watch this online someday.

And every other human being on this planet.

Just so that I am clear, You are the Billionaire that I am speaking of.

I am not talking about dollars, euros, pesos, or British pounds even. Nothing you can touch or see. Yet you can spend it still the same.

All you have to do is believe in the power of one small word -We.

II

Let me tell you my story.

I was born in 1968 when the world was also falling apart.

Martin Luther King was fighting for racial equality; Nelson Mandela against Apartheid; Gloria Steinem, Women's Rights; the Gay Rights movement was beginning; there was a global flu pandemic; and the US was in Vietnam.

As a child, everyone around me seemed to be fighting. But instead of fighting, I was dreaming

And I had big dreams.

Dreams of inventing. Dreams of traveling the world. Dreams of starting companies. My phoenix was rising.

III

Many people thought my dreams were fantasy back then. There were so few examples of it in the 70s, for any race or any gender, and especially for a young black girl.

But I knew that my dreams mattered (and your dreams matter) and that they were possible, with The Power of the We.

All reality starts in the imagination. Beliefs have creative power. And here are mine as a kid and as an adult.

IV

First, I believe that we are all connected in this world through God. Could I do it alone?- No. Could We do it together?- Yes.

Second, I believe in the currency of Faith. And I spent Faith vigilantly, by telling everyone and anyone the story of the future that I imagined. I knew my believers existed somewhere in this world. I just had to find them

Yes, Yes, Yes, I needed a lot of miracles! And they came- in the form of other people, showing up at the right moment, in the right way. Mentors, Co-Founders, Investors, Customers...We made me the success that I am today.

V

I got degrees from Cornell and Harvard, and co-founded seven startups with The Power of the We.

From a ticket business, to a backpack company; to digital satellite radio; to a healthcare clinic in Ethiopia, that has treated thousands of patients; to a broadband company; to a Virtual Reality gaming platform; to Tribetan, an ed-tech and innovation literacy company today.

I have seen the world. I have been to over fifty countries, including South Africa in the 90s, after the end of Apartheid. I had the pleasure of working with then President Nelson Mandela.

"It all seems impossible until it is done."

That little girl in me never gave up on her imagination. Not then, not now and not tomorrow. And please don't give up on yours. Your imagination is how God prays to You.

"The power of storytelling is the ability to create reality itself."
Tiffany Norwood

THAT TREE IN
THE FOREST

Imagine a young black woman in her 20s, with micro braids down the middle of her back, looking like a college student, saying that she wants to build some satellites. And then *raising nearly a billion dollars*, to do it. I mean, c'mon.

We live in a narrative based existence. The power of storytelling is the ability to create reality itself.

You know that philosophical question: *Did the tree make a sound when it fell in the forest if no one was there to hear it?* That question is irrelevant, and so is the answer.

The real question is this: *Did the tree make a sound or even exist at all, if no one talked about it, or told the story of it?* Or what if they lie and say no forest, no tree, no sound.

II

The story is the reality, even if it is not the truth. She (or he) who can tell a good story- Can raise money, rule countries, and control the truth.

When I raised the $670 million for WorldSpace, Noah, the founder, had already been trying to do it for a couple of years. The guys on the team were older than me by nearly twenty years.

Their story was weighty with talk about broadcast licenses, compression technology, system architecture, and project plans. The setting was the nineties, before iTunes or Google. The dream was so radical; we needed more story and less pitch. The guys might have been older than me, but I was the only one with experience doing a startup.

III

My narrative went something like this: What if we can talk to each other. What happens if we redistribute the truth? South Africa sharing stories with the US, Canada sharing stories with Japan, France sharing stories with Chile. Not the governments, not big business. Us, you and me. What would that world look like?

We are going to launch three satellites to cover every country on earth. Alcatel will be our general contractor.
And when we are done, the world will be able to speak to the world.
In the form of news,
In the form of sports,
In the form of music and entertainment.

It will change everything.

And it did.

PERSUASIVE STORYTELLING FOR CHANGEMAKERS

I have a group of friends who are writers of fiction. They talk in genres like Romance or Thrillers. I told them mine is "Speculative Reality." And yes, I invented it.

Persuasive storytelling is essential for changemakers. It is different than reporting like a journalist, or entertaining, like a screenwriter. It is more of a hybrid of the creative and the objective. A story crafted and told in such a way that it inspires people to take action -to invest, to partner, to join the team, to buy a product.

I spend hours, sometimes days and weeks even, teaching persuasive storytelling to executives, students, founders and changemakers. Connection is the primary directive. Here is a very quick over-view.

Let's begin with the universal languages
of persuasion and influence: conviction, objectiv-ity, and grace.

II

Conviction in words and gestures shows that the idea is important to you. It is being definitive, "I will do this." instead of "I feel I might do something, maybe." Having high energy and authenticity. Con-necting your life, interests, and background to the mission. Conviction makes it clear that to the audi-ence that you will not give up.

Objectivity in pictures, case studies, prototypes, data... demonstrates that the idea is rooted in real-ity. It's not just a passion project. Objectivity shows that the dream has true potential in the real world.

And lastly, but most importantly, Grace. Grace es-tablishes the value of the product, service or idea to others:
-by solving a problem
-by providing delight
-by being of service.

Grace should eventually be so high, and so obvious

in the story, that others are willing to pay for it or donate to it. Some of the dialects of grace are case studies, testimonials, and of course, having actual customers. It is a list of benefits instead of features.

III

Let's talk about the difference between benefits and features. "It runs on the MySQL database."

That is a feature.

"You will have access to your data, everywhere and anywhere, on any device, 24/7. It will be at your fingertips, when and where you need it."

Those are benefits.

Another way to look at it is like this:
-Conviction is You
-Objectivity is the Product, Service or Company
-Grace is about the Customer

Ultimately, it is a persuasive narrative, not a pitch.

IV

I judge a lot of startup contests and work with a lot of founders. The best stories have balance. The worst don't. Generally, they are heavy on the objectivity. The narrative is more about the product instead of the customer. And the audience has no idea why they, in particular, should be the One to do it.

If the sole motivation for bringing your idea to life is money, then when there is fire (and there is always fire), you will most likely give up. Products and companies don't fail. People do.

No one wants to give money or time to something that won't last. Give yourself a score on each of the three languages of influence. The goal is to have nearly an equal amount of Conviction, Objectivity, and Grace.

First, write out your narrative as an essay.
In the beginning, don't worry about the Power-Point. When you are in that proverbial elevator, you will not have time to pull out a preso.

The story always comes first.

Start the story with Conviction and Grace. Conviction and Grace establish a connection to you and the idea. Your audience must care, to listen to the Objectivity facts and figures. Attention is a gift.

V

Ultimately, your goal is for the story to leave the room. For it to go viral, in the analog. To create your own luck. Where the next thing you know, a person named Mary sends you a message saying:

"James told me about that cool thing you are working on. I am interested."

For that to happen, the story has to be both compelling
and simple enough that your audience will share it with others.

Test the story on family and friends to see if they can retell it. That's your proxy. That's your feedback loop. This storytelling framework works whenever you need to be persuasive. Not just for startups.

Now that you have that first story, tell it everywhere and anywhere. Tell it to anyone that will listen to find your believers.

"Successful people don't waste opportunities to be heard or counted."

Tiffany Norwood

VOTE LIKE A BOSS

I am not saying it was as easy as just telling a story.
I had to tell the story a thousand times to someone
else's hundred. While at the same time, being called
the N-word, the B-word, and the C-word.

I have been called the whole alphabet.

I would not wish the attacks I have faced on anyone.

The lemonade of it all is this- those attacks readied
me at the age of 27 to raise $670 million dollars for a
startup. Which no one of any age or gender had done
before or since.

II

Was it hard? Yes, of course, it was hard. But isn't living *without* your dreams hard too?

So yes, I have suffered.

I've lost money.
I've lost health.
I've lost sleep.

I have been treated terribly for being black, for being a woman, and many many many years ago, for being too young.

Where is the 50 over 50 list to watch?
Because I am just getting started!

Fear, anxiety and panic, have all been my best friends.

Your dreams are not free.
Why should they be?

Suffering is the price to pay.
Patience a virtue.
And winning the best response.

Winning at your dreams.
Winning at school.
Winning at work.
Winning at sports.
Winning at seeing the world.
Winning at raising money.
Winning with a patent issued!
And, winning with the right to vote

III

I mentioned this because recently, I was asked to give a talk about- How has the right to Vote impacted me? For an entrepreneur, we know it's an unusual request, the organizer added.

I do have thoughts on that.
I have been journaling about it for years.

What they didn't know was that I was the first in my family to be born with all of my civil rights.

Happy 100th to the 19th Amendment, giving most women the right to vote. And Happy 55th to the Voting Rights Act. I needed both.

Let me ask you a question that I have asked myself many times. Could I have been an entrepreneur, inventor and leader, if I didn't have the right to vote? It was hard enough, even with my civil rights. Let's be clear:

Laws don't change people's behavior.
Time does.

IV

As far as I know, I am the only successful black female tech entrepreneur that started companies in my era.

The journey has been extraordinary. Women weren't even allowed to have their own bank accounts when I was a child. Let alone their own companies.

Being a founder, inventor and leader has been truly miraculous.

Could I have done all those things if every couple of years my country made it very clear that
My opinion,
My point of view,
My ideas, and
My VOTE did not matter?

What impact would that have had on my mindset?
How would that have affected my imagination?

I grew up with parents that supported my ideas. My Mom and Dad were my biggest believers. Mom is in the audience today!

I also was included in the Constitution.

I had God.

I needed all of the above to strengthen my imagination. To believe in myself. To create.

It was excruciatingly hard. It was lonely. In the beginning, I had few mentors. No one wanted the black girl there in the first place. My friends could not relate to nor fully understand what I was doing.

You are going to build satellites? What?

My magic was taking place behind closed doors, alone in rooms full of powerful men.

If one of those elements were missing (like my civil rights), who knows if the outcomes would have been the same. Even with the cover of the constitution, I have to spend an incomparable amount of time on issues of equality and abuse of power that my male counterparts don't have to deal with. And still be competitive and high performing in a space that is, by nature, intense, fast-paced and challenging.

Could I have been that bold in thought and deed, if I was being told my vote, and therefore my opinions don't count?

V

Voting is more than laws and policies and candidates. I have been to over fifty countries. I was in post-apartheid South Africa twenty-five years ago.

I watched firsthand the effort, joy and violence of trying to build a democracy from scratch.

I was also in Venezuela in 1990-1991. I witnessed firsthand the struggle, division and violence of the dismantling of a democracy when Chavez came to power.

VI

From Turkey to the now non-existent Yugoslavia, my being out in the world as an entrepreneur gave me a unique up-close perspective on the life and death of freedom.

Which is this-

Democracy is fragile.
Democracy is a team sport.

Democracy is the sum of all the people of a society and how much they care about each other; and how much they care about themselves.

You need both to create a democracy.
And you need both to maintain it.

VII

I use to travel thousands of miles to cast my ballot.

They were long (and expensive) international flights.

I was like, "I have to get home to vote!"
I was like, "My vote will change everything!"

My invention will change everything!
My business idea will change everything!
My opinion will change everything!

Isn't it all the same thing? Isn't it about taking your-self seriously? Like when you raise your hand in class, like when you speak up to family, friends and colleagues; and, like when you Vote.

Aren't they all similar personal traits you need to practice to be successful in business, school, sports, and life?

My vote matters,
My ideas matter,
My invention matters.
My new way,
My different way,
My better way,
Matters.

I am talking about a growth mindset. I am talking about voting as an act of self-worth, self-respect...a practice of leadership.

If you don't think your vote matters, how will you ever believe your dreams, ideas or opinions matter?

Successful people don't waste opportunities to be heard or counted.

Vote Like A Boss.

"Life is not the time to wait."
Tiffany Norwood

ASTOUND YOURSELF

Thomas Edison once said, if we did everything we were capable of, we would astound ourselves.

Take yourself seriously.
Astound yourself, like Patricia Bath.

She was the daughter of a father who was an immigrant from Trinidad. Her mother was a descendant of slaves and worked as a housekeeper.

Patricia Bath was a black female innovator.
She was the pioneer of laser cataract surgery.
An activist against blindness.
A Howard University graduate.

She was an inventor who holds five patents.
Know her name.

Ms. Bath died last year, ironically not living to see 2020.
The Year of Vision.

Her year.

I wanted to salute her publicly.
To make sure the world knew her story.
To encourage you to see how far conviction and grace can take you.

Patricia Bath was relentless in fulfilling her calling to help people See.

She didn't wait for the world to take her imagination seriously.

She did it herself.

Astound yourself, like Patricia Bath.
Life is not the time to wait.

My dream is to see Patricia Bath inducted into the Inventors Hall of Fame. Her impact on the precious gift of vision has been tremendous.

Now let's also <u>honor</u> it.

"God believes in you. Do you believe in yourself?"
Tiffany Norwood

THE POWER OF WE 2.0

Know your Power, and use it. And also know that you can't do it alone.

Even inventors who hold patents, people who literally have done things that no other person has done before, can not do it alone.

Less than three percent of patents make it to market. And if you take away the pharmaceuticals, less than one percent are financially successful.

The risk of someone else stealing your work, taking it to market and being wildly successful, is less than one percent.

Good news, right?

The bad news is that those are your odds too.

Unless you collaborate, in the form of Co-Founders, partners, mentors, and more.

File for a patent or trademark, the USPTO website and tools make it so much easier now. And then, move on.

II

Know that from that small, tiny place of Me, You immediately put yourself in a box, as a person or as a country.

One person's mind.
One collection of resources,
One pile of money.

But, from that powerful place of We, You and your believers. It is not only possible; it's doable. From inventing the better way, to starting a company, to changing the world.

You are a Billionaire with the We.

More than one million in the DC metro area,
300 million in the US
600 million in Latin America
700 million in Europe
1 billion in Africa
4 billion in Asia

Over 7 Billion in the World!

In the currency of Faith and connection,

You have billions in your bank account
Right here, right now, today.

You are a Billionaire.

Good news right-
Worthy and Wealthy

Now, here is the most important question you will
ever ask yourself.

How are you going to spend it?
How are you going to spend Faith?

III

I pray for you, your family, your community, your
country and the world, that you spend it on your
dreams.

Don't be selfish. We need your imagination more
than ever.

We are all in this together. All you need is one or two
others, at moments along the way to get it all done.
One believer turns into a few, hundreds, thousands,
millions.

Miracles happen through other people.
And there are billions of us in this world.

Tell your story. Just take the first step, by saying, with Faith, to anyone that will listen-

I Have a Dream.

Can you feel it?
It's a feeling, not a thinking.
Can you feel it, my fellow Changemakers?

God believes in You.
Do You believe in Yourself?

"The world may attack your genius now, but love you for it later."
Tiffany Norwood

THAT UNICORN

I want to close with a poem celebrating a fearless female leader that embodies everything I shared today.

She is better than any unicorn.

I promised we would talk about cats, Billionaires, storytelling, and unicorns. I didn't forget.

Who came up with the term, a Unicorn to signify an entrepreneur who has hit it big?

I can't imagine it was an actual entrepreneur, innovator or inventor who first used it.

Founders are self-made.

We don't just appear in forests, with a horn sticking out of our heads, born of unicorn parents.

There is, however, something otherworldly (and insane) about us Founder types.

And it is this-
We spend all of our savings, and sometimes nearly (actually) lose our homes; while working sixteen hours a day to be of service to our team, customers, and investors.

If we endure (and that is a huge if), we eventually find mastery. First of ourselves and then of the enterprise and the market.

And maybe five or more years later, we are cashflow positive.

How is that similar to a unicorn?

It is more like the origin story of Hermione.

Yes, from Harry Potter.

My closing will be a poem called "Hermione Rising."

Hermione is a role model for all of us. The so-called muggle who from sheer will and creative power-recognizes, practices and masters her magic within and then goes on to be of exceptional service to others.

Someday I am sure there will be a Herman Granger.

Hermione is all of us.

"Reality is always messy. Screw up, and then Rise up."
Tiffany Norwood

HERMIONE RISING

I imagine a new way, a different way...

I imagine a Better Way!

Something disruptive and innovative.
Used and revered.
Demanded and paid for
Something...transformative.

II

Imagination,
Why do we deny it?
  Or discount it?
It is the source of all innovation.

Einstein was theoretical, not applied.
Davinci, an artist and a scientist.
George Washington Carver,

no vision, no hope.

And Harriett had to have imagined freedom,
    before she took the first step.

III

I Have a Dream!
-of traveling to space
-of curing cancer
-of starting companies
-of running for office
-of peace, unity, equality,
And Equity.

You get what I am saying.

IV

It is not about the How.
It's about the Why.
The sense of purpose.
The Calling.

No need to teach imagination.
Just endorse it.
And with grace, give space for it.

It's not to be packed away.
It should be on display.

In schools, in offices,
A priority among the others.

Serious vote
For tinkering,
For sketching
For making, and
For play.

Forcing memorization,
Of someone else's prior imagination,
 is not the way.

V

The recipe-
Give space to expand
 and extend a concept.

Through empathy and understanding.
Through diversity and collaboration.
 an embrace for imagination,
In the case of them all.

The more minds that imagine together,
The more innovation blossoms.
The more diverse these minds,
The taller it grows.
And if It's fueled by love
 and understanding,
It thrives and soars.

We are 7 billion strong,
Brothers and Sisters.
We can do anything.
Unless we fight each other.

Go Human or Go Home!

VI

(Day) Dreamers,
You are our future game-changers,
Your place is at the top of the class.
Take out your wand,
And cast the spell of

"I Want That"

It is going to be messy.
Reality is always messy.
Screw up and then,
Rise Up!

Wield the magic of Hope and Faith.

And know that the world
    may attack your genius now,
But love you for it later.

Hermione is Rising,
    and her power is limitless.

By God's grace,
So is yours.

At this moment in history,
    more than ever,
I pray you will use it
    for the greater good.

Amen.

::: INSPIRATION :::

A PRAYER FOR
THOSE INSPIRED

Dear Voter,

You have embarked on a powerful journey.

It began when you received the charge to vote for your future - your dreams. Of course, you could have taken a different path (or you could have rejected this charge altogether). But you received this charge. And when you did, you stepped out in Faith toward not only on what could lie ahead for you; you took a leap of Faith toward what could lie ahead for each one of us.

Because you see, Dear Voter, when you determined to believe in what is possible for yourself, you inherently claimed agency for what is possible for all people - each one of us interconnected to all others from the beginning of time to its end. In other words, when you received the charge to vote for your future, you expanded the boundaries of hope for all people, as with each forward movement, each positive act; each breath of encouragement you take, eternity takes a much larger form. In this way, not only does your life have renewed meaning, so does mine.

Thank you.

At this moment in our story ever-unfolding, I invite you to join me in prayer.

A Prayer for Those Inspired
to Vote Like a Boss

Author of Life and Source of All Goodness,
    We praise you for the glories of this day.

For our privilege to learn from one another,
    We praise you.

For the ones who have nurtured and supported, informed and encouraged us,
    We praise you.

For the diverse gifts and abilities you have awakened in each one of us,
    We praise you.

For the opportunity to change the trajectory of the universe through our hard-earned right to vote,

We give you thanks and praise.

As we reflect upon the state of our nation
And the demands of us that lie ahead,
We ask that you seal our commitment
To be a part of much needed change.

In a nation of conflict,
　　　May our votes help to bring about peace.

In a nation of discord,
　　　May our votes stimulate unity.

In a nation of self-indulgence,
　　　May our votes encourage generosity.

In a nation of despair,
　　　May our votes lead to hope.

In a nation of anger,
　　　May our votes compel us to love.

In a nation of disrespect,
　　　May our votes create a way for honor.

In a nation of hubris,
　　　May our votes affirm the value of humility.

In a nation of disapproval,
　　　May our votes create a way for grace.

In a nation of sadness,
>   May our votes create a way for joy.

In a nation of outrageous want,
>   May our votes create a way
>   for each one of us

To offer ourselves as a holy embodiment of your
will,
Intent upon expanding the boundaries of hope

For all eternity.

As we each cast our votes this year (and the next),

May we continue to feel inspired to live into a full-
ness
That only You could know.

May we embrace the transformations we have
undergone
>   And the developments
We will someday know.

May we grow from the opportunities we have
missed
>   Or the mistakes we have made along the way.

And as we move through the stages of our life,
May we reflect with gladness upon the years we

have been a part of much needed change, and be content that our involvement was time well spent.

Yes, thanks be to You,
        O Author of life,
And all praise to You
For the glories of our days.

May You be a persistently felt spirit among us

As our constant companion and guide.

Amen.

The Reverend Beverly Dempsey
New York City

BLACK LIVES MATTER

As a school student, I always questioned my parents about why we were separated. Why can't we go there? I would ask. My parents said this is how the white leaders designed the country. They wanted slaves, not citizens. And then, after slavery, they wanted servants to be controlled by their white bosses. Their goal was never for us to be equal under the law. It was ours.

As business owners, my parents encouraged us to speak up and to write articles about equality to our teachers. My parents always told us to find peaceful ways to talk about our concerns.

That sparked in me the desire to march and to protest. Our all-black school allowed us to make posters and to march on campus. When Rosa Parks refused to move to the back of a city bus, I joined a march in support of her. And later, I even attended the *March on Washington* for jobs and freedom.

To help me to learn more, I studied and wrote papers about the first Civil Rights Act of 1964, the Voting Rights Act of 1965, and the Civil Rights Act of 1968. Black Lives Matter.

And I always voted. I remember every election. The most memorable being when I voted to help elect Barak Obama. I felt so blessed to have lived long enough in this world to help select the first black president of the United States of America. I felt that my parents, who are in heaven, were celebrating his election too.

We live in Washington, DC, and on the evening that he won the election, my daughter Tiffany and I walked the streets of our capital. The city was filled with people celebrating while making their way down to the White House. They were all races, genders, and ages. In my decades of living in this city, I had seen nothing like it.

We spontaneously gathered in joy all night in front of the White House, until almost daybreak. My daughter and I then walked home. She had to catch a flight for a work trip. I was so excited. I couldn't go to sleep. So instead, I went home, ate some breakfast, and then immediately headed out again. I bought up all the newspapers I could find, for my family and friends. I bought souvenirs and magazines. To this day, I have a box filled with special things about him and his family.

That January, we went to his Inauguration and the parade. All the beautiful streets of Washington were filled with happy people from all over the country and around the world to honor President Barack Obama, the First Lady, Michelle Obama, and their daughters, Sasha and Malia. All walking united to this special historical event. It was an extraordinary experience, one of the best of my life.

I taught my children the importance of voting at a very young age. We would often discuss world events and politics, especially during an election year. As soon as they reached the age to vote, they registered. I educated my children about why it was important to be counted. That their opinion matters. That even with imperfect choices, staying silent in an election never works. That elections have consequences, good and bad. That it is imperative always to vote.

Mary Ann Norwood
Washington, DC

THE KINDNESS OF STRANGERS

A core message of many of the writings in *Vote Like a Boss* is "The Power of We." You can't do it alone. The very first element of the Tribetan Method, my framework for innovation, focuses on the Core Beliefs required for the Tribetan Method to work. Namely (1) that we are all connected in this world and (2) that other people will help you. That's it, just those two requirements to get started.

You would think that would be good news (and it is), but immediately people begin to question, How are we all connected? Who will show up? Why will they help? Do I have to believe in God? The good news is that skepticism is OK. The critical thing is that just for this particular experience, you believe that we are all connected. Even if how is a great mystery. Believe that other people, yes even strangers, will show up to help along the way. Spiritual belief is optional.

If you look back on your own life, you will see that you have already had many instances of feeling overwhelmed and someone showing up to help out. Investing time, pointing the way, or giving you just the advice you needed to get the job done. When you have a moment, write down a story of when a stranger helped you when you needed it most.

Then write a simple thank you to that person, and if you are able, send it to them. Approach your goals and dreams, trusting that you will not have to do it alone. Believing that people will show up again. And with this Faith, demonstrate your pro-active gratitude by being of service today to help others achieve theirs. We can get through this pandemic and the uncertainty, if we do it together. Visit www.Tribetan.com to learn more about the Tribetan Method.

Tiffany Ann Norwood
Washington, DC

"God will never let you fail or fall."
Mary Ann Norwood

::: FINAL THOUGHTS :::

AFTERWORD

It was an absolute honor to be the first keynote speaker in the ten-year history of the USPTO Women's Entrepreneurship Symposium. We learned, laughed, and cried together; and, I will forever hold dear the standing ovation you gave me. I was told that this happens with rare occasions, and I am humbled.

I used this one-hour platform to make a case for success as a human science and inclusive innovation as smart business. I advocated for the importance of imagination and taking your dreams seriously. I made a plea for inventor Patricia Bath to be inducted into the Inventors Hall of Fame and shared her unbelievable story. I taught the basics of Persuasive Storytelling and encouraged people to share theirs. I talked about why voting is an act of self-worth and how I could not have been an inventor or an entrepreneur without the 19th Amendment.

This keynote was also my last live speech. It was

an inspiring gathering of people passionate about changing the world one invention at a time. I spent hours catching up with the audience after my performance and was blown away by their stories and innovations. And many asked me to autograph the ToPAQ patent! I was in inventor heaven! Thank you to everyone at the USPTO for such a great event.

Vote Like a Boss is that speech, plus other writings, essays, and poems inspired by the performance and the act of voting.

Tiffany Ann Norwood
Washington, DC

"You are worthy and wealthy. How are you going to spend faith?"
Tiffany Norwood

MORE VOTE LIKE
A BOSS

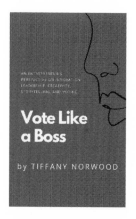

Watch live performances of "Hermione Rising"and of "The Power of We." Check out cool merchandise and more at VoteLikeABoss.com. Learn more about Tiffany's story at www.TiffanyNorwood.com. Tell us what you thought of *Vote Like a Boss*, please use this link to share your feedback. For inquiries, contact Hello@Tribetan.com.

ABOUT TIFFANY NORWOOD

In the 1990s, Tiffany Norwood did something that no other entrepreneur has done since -she raised over $670 million dollars to fund a startup. She was 27 at the time. That money was used to build the first-ever global digital radio platform; launch three satellites into space, including XM Radio; support the development of MP3/MP4 technologies, and invest in a new generation of digital radio receivers. As one of the few global serial entrepreneurs and the first successful black female tech entrepreneur, Ms. Norwood's career has spanned 52 countries, 30+ years, 7 startups, and a patent. She was also the first in her family to be born with all of their civil rights.

Tiffany did her first startup as a teenager and had a patent by the age of twenty-three. Her ventures have ranged from the first one-strap backpack to the automation technology behind self-install kits for broadband internet, and a virtual reality gaming platform. She also led some of the first-ever digital content licensing deals, including Bloomberg News and CNN International. Tiffany was also an early collaborator with the Fraunhofer Institute and their MPEG technologies.

Currently, Tiffany is the Founder and CEO of Tribetan. Tribetan teaches everyone entrepreneurship and innovation literacy for success in business, school, and life. With modules on Persuasive Storytelling, Cultivated Endurance, How to Practice, and The Power of We and the human science of success.

Venues have included the European Parliament, Yale, the USPTO, KMPG, Bishop McNamara High School, University of South Carolina, the South African Embassy, and many more. Tribetan's mission is that the science of turning imagination into reality, is as well-known as reading, writing, and math. Tiffany recently published her first book, *Vote Like a Boss*.

Tiffany has an MBA from Harvard and a Bachelor's in Economics with a concentration in statistics and electrical engineering from Cornell University.

You can connect with @TiffanyNorwood on Instagram, Twitter and LinkedIn.

"Is the Cat alive or dead?"